A Little Monster's

GUIDE TO POSITIVITY

A LITTLE MONSTER'S GUIDE TO POSITIVITY

An Hachette UK Company
www.hachette.co.uk

Vie Books, an imprint of Summersdale Publishers Ltd
Part of Octopus Publishing Group Limited
Carmelite House
50 Victoria Embankment
LONDON
EC4Y 0DZ
UK

www.summersdale.com

Printed and bound in China

ISBN: 978-1-80007-724-9

Substantial discounts on bulk quantities of Summersdale books are available to corporations, professional associations and other organizations. For details contact general enquiries: telephone: +44 (0) 1243 771107 or email: enquiries@summersdale.com.

Neither the author nor the publisher can be held responsible for any loss or claim arising out of the use, or misuse, of the suggestions made herein. None of the views or suggestions in this book are intended to replace medical opinion from a doctor. If you have concerns about your health or that of a child in your care, please seek advice from a medical professional.

A Little Monster's
GUIDE TO POSITIVITY

Emily Snape

Note to parents and carers

This book will help your child to:

- find out why they have negative feelings and learn how to let them go

- be kind to themselves with positive self-talk

- feel calmer and happier with some simple and effective techniques.

These approaches can become powerful tools that will encourage your child to feel happier and more resilient.

Hi!

It's great to meet you.

I'm Fluff and sometimes my emotions get in the way of having fun. I don't always feel like I'm good enough and sometimes things are just tooooo tricky.

So, with the help of my monster friends, I'm going to explore all sorts of ways to be MORE positive so I can make the most of EVERY day and achieve whatever I want to.

I'd love you to be part of my exciting POSITIVE journey!

These are my friends:

Goo

Spike

Nala

Imani

Kalina

Yuze

What do you say to a three-headed monster? Hello, hello, hello!

It can make me feel a bit miserable when I think about how much hairier and scarier and slimier they all are than me.

But Goo (the ghost) says I'm ONE-OF-A-KIND.

In fact we are all completely UNIQUE and that's actually totally awesome!

Goo suggested I celebrate being ME by thinking about what makes ME special...

So, I gave it some thought and here's what I discovered:

My favourite and least favourite foods

YUMMY	YUCKY
BOOberry pie	SANDwiches
Spookghetti	Bubble and squeak
Eyes cream and jellyfish	ROCK cakes
Mice Crispies	Bangers and mash
Lightbulbs (for a light snack)	
Ghoulslaw	
Fish and Ships	

My best outfit:

Snake scarf

Tap shoes

My stinkiest socks!

What I love to do:

Have a mud bath

Play squash

Laugh my head off

Play Where's the Werewolf?

Eat an eyeball surprise

Play BATmington

What about you?

But one of the things that gets me down is that I am the ONLY monster I know who can't shout "Boo".

When I try it comes out as a little squeak.

boo.

I get so nervous that everyone will laugh at me when they hear how quiet my "Boo!" is and next week it is SPOOKING day where you spend the entire day shouting "BOO!"

I'm very worried about it.

A mean voice in my head tells me I'm no good and that Spooking day will be a disaster.

We all have emotions. Some make us feel good and others don't. When I'm really WORRIED this is what happens to me...

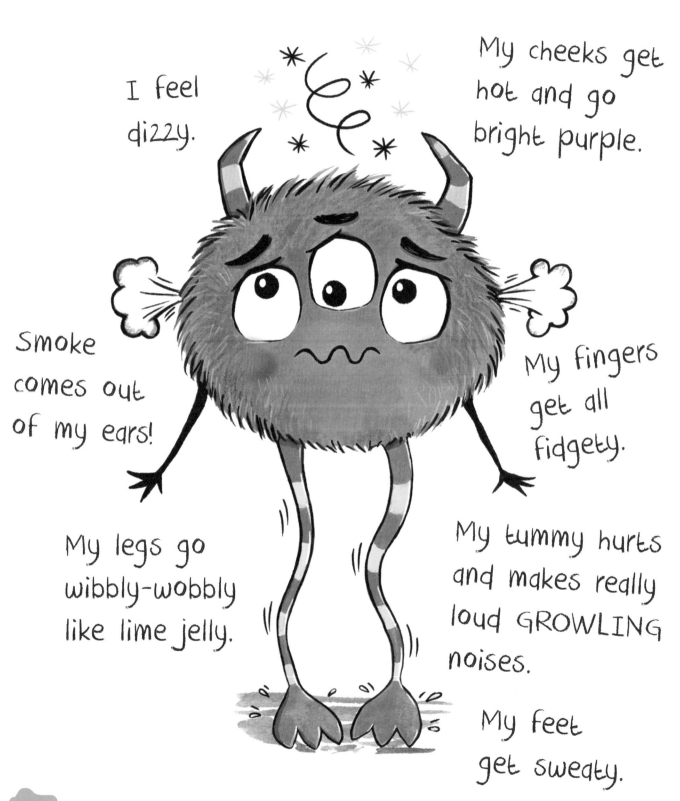

I feel dizzy.

My cheeks get hot and go bright purple.

Smoke comes out of my ears!

My fingers get all fidgety.

My legs go wibbly-wobbly like lime jelly.

My tummy hurts and makes really loud GROWLING noises.

My feet get sweaty.

When I feel worried, I am sometimes unkind to my friends.

And that makes me feel even worse.

All emotions are important and necessary but sometimes how we feel might be getting in the way of what we want to do. If you are feeling worried, sad, angry or jealous and your emotion is overwhelming you, there are LOTS of simple ways to take back control...

These are Goo's suggestions...

Goo's Top Tips to cool down

1. Take calming breaths.

2. Slowly count to TEN.

3. Focus on looking around and spotting all your favourite colours.

4. Hum a tune in your head.

When I tried Goo's ideas, it really helped.

Breathe...

Deep breathing tips:

Get into a comfortable position. Lie on the floor, sit down or stand up, whatever suits you.

Try breathing in through your nose while counting to five. Then slowly let the air flow gently out of your mouth while counting to seven.

I asked my other friends if they had any ways to make themselves feel more positive too...

Spike says there's no point blaming others over how you are feeling. Instead, try going outside and relaxing on the grass.

Nala says what gets her in a better mood is making some art.

I'm painting my sister!

Imani finds listening to music helps him.

Kalina says she feels good by doing some exercise.

If you still feel unhappy, there's ALWAYS something you can do about it.

Goo said to try talking to someone I trust, so I made a drawing of my friends and family I can tell my worries to:

My teacher

Nana Misty

Mum

Who's on your list?

18

I told Nana Misty about how terrible I am at shouting "BOO!"

She listened carefully, then explained that everyone starts out as a beginner and not to be afraid to try. Instead of worrying about what might go wrong, take little steps to feel more confident at new challenges.

So, I've been practising and practising and now I've got pretty good at it!

I've started writing a "gratitude journal" of all the things I am thankful for and it's helped me realize that even when things seem bad, there is actually LOTS to feel happy and positive about.

You could try one too?

Fluff's Gratitude List

1. My home. It's small and squelchy and stinks, just how I like it.

2. My family. I wouldn't be here without them!

3. My friends who make me laugh my head off. Literally. It rolled down the hill last week.

4. Jumping in muddy puddles!

5. My favourite books.

6. Hairy hugs!

And I'm making plans of things I'd like to do so I have lots to look forward to.

I even asked Nana Misty if we can spend Spooking Day together next week!

I am really grateful my friends have done so much to help me feel more positive and I wanted to say thank you, so I made them some boiled slug and mud cupcakes.

I also wanted to apologize to Yuze for taking my emotions out on her.

And the thing is, being kind to others actually made me feel even better about myself, TOO!

Yuze said she forgave me and also explained it is really important to look after yourself. If you are healthy, then everything will feel better.

She said it is really important to:

Drink enough water...

I find it really tricky to get to sleep, so I worked hard on making my bedroom comfortable and relaxing.

And I even sorted out my books.

Cyclops
I. C. Huw

SNAKES BY ANNA CONDA

OUCH! By A. B. Stung

A NIGHT IN THE HAUNTED HOUSE
ELIZA WAKE

Rodent in the House!
E. K. Mouse

I'm feeling a lot more positive about EVERYTHING. I can overcome challenges, try new things, and if something doesn't go well, I can learn from it!

We are ALL wonderful and totally ROARSOME! Thank you so much for helping me on my POSITIVE journey. I hope you FEEL GREAT about yourself too.

You are AMAZING and can do ANYTHING YOU PUT YOUR MIND TO!

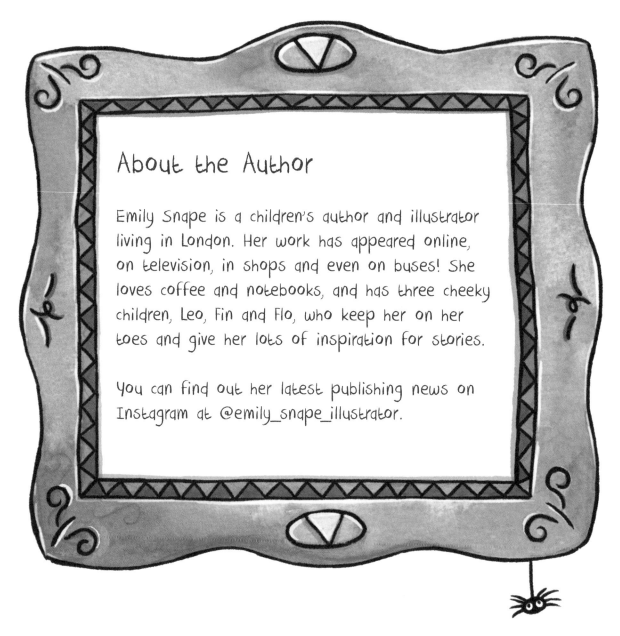

About the Author

Emily Snape is a children's author and illustrator living in London. Her work has appeared online, on television, in shops and even on buses! She loves coffee and notebooks, and has three cheeky children, Leo, Fin and Flo, who keep her on her toes and give her lots of inspiration for stories.

You can find out her latest publishing news on Instagram at @emily_snape_illustrator.

If you're interested in finding out more about our books, find us on Facebook at **Summersdale Publishers**, on Twitter at **@Summersdale** and on Instagram and TikTok at **@summersdalebooks** and get in touch.

We'd love to hear from you!

Thanks very much for buying this Summersdale book.

www.summersdale.com